New Wine Skins:

Transforming tomorrow's church…
Today.

By Damien S. Fields

Copyright © 2016

By Damien S, Fields

Cover Art by: Tris Beezley

www.trisbeezley.com

Publisher HMP Inc.

P.O. Box 4142

Chapel Hill NC.27514

Printed & Published in the United States

ISBN - 13: 978- 1533148209

ISBN - 10: 1533148201

Table of Contents

Foreword

This book was created as a practical guide, designed for today's non-profit organizational leader. In it, offers admonition against the unnecessary yet common pitfalls and errors that often occur within this industry. As a matter of fact, the principles and practices discussed, can be utilized by any leader and if implement, are sure to make a beneficial difference toward efficiency and performance within your organization.

Introduction

Non-profit organizations are businesses with specific needs and requirements. The typical for-profit business is focused on profits and losses, while a non-profit business is focused on societal purposes, benefits and organizational missions. Researchers have discovered that non-profit business has expanded over the years and continues to expand as they experience greater financial growth, innovation and technological advancement.

Non-profit organizations have unique ways of governance that are different than For-profit businesses but also have some striking financial and organizational similarities.

In non-profit governance, at the Board level of management, is the heart of decision making for the business (Mckinney, 2015). The study of Board of Trustee members and their efficiency and performance is a viable business problem within churches and non-profit organizations of all sizes in today's society. According to Berman (2015) efficiency and performance is not only important to for-profit organizations but also to the agenda of non-profit organizations. This book focuses on what I believe to be three foundational strategies and concepts that Board of Trustee members need to have, to effectively accomplish their organizational goals and purposes.

Now at the end of the day, there is no quick fix as a solution to any problem. Although it has been proven that good efforts toward better practice, will certainly lead to improvement. The following three implementations, seek to encourage that.

The Right Ingredients

The making of wine has a unique process. It involves fermented grapes or other fruits. Due to a natural chemical balance, grapes ferment without the addition of sugars, acids, enzymes, water, or other nutrients. Yeast consumes the sugar in the grapes and converts it to ethanol and carbon dioxide. Different varieties of grapes and strains of yeasts produce different styles of wine. These variations result from the complex interactions between the biochemical development of the grape, the reactions involved in fermentation, the terroir (the special characteristics imparted by geography, geology, climate and plant genetics) and subsequent appellation (the legally defined and protected geographical indication used to identify where the grapes for a wine were grown), along with human intervention in the overall process (Herriaz, 1990).

Sounds complicated huh? Nonetheless, no matter how complicated or simple they are, the right ingredients are critical in making wine and also in Non-profit leadership. The mixture of balance of theocracy and bureaucracy is needed in having the right ingredients. Board of Trustee's in theory are supposed to be members that assist the organization with decision making and pushing forward the mission of the church or non-profit organization. As I mentioned, having the right ingredients is key. So what are the right ingredients? I believe the right ingredients are as follows;

A. Him or her who has a proven track record or displays a desire for social good or change. Remember, most Non-profit religious organizations or Churches have non-paid positions.

B. Him or her who has a proven track record or displays a desire for excellence and commitment.

C. Him or her who has a proven track record or displays experience in a related field.

I believe it is important that right ingredients are chosen not because he or she is a friend of the Church or Non-profit organization, but because they are good fit for the organization's mission and societal purpose. In Board membership it is important that the right ingredients exist. The right ingredients are not perfect but they are right for the situation. When choosing a Board member, the non-profit agency must sure that the prospective candidates must be right for the organizations culture and current situation. Past situations cannot be standards or measurements for which are used to assess the viability of a possible candidate. I pray this chapter empowers and encourage your organizations to make sure you have the right ingredients. Below are some positive and negative examples of the Right Ingredients.

Positive Example: *Board of Trustees in a Church in the Raleigh-Durham area of North Carolina is deliberating on a very important decision concerning a major real* *estate purchase. Though the Board does not always agree they are willing to come to non-bias consensus that move forward the agenda of the major real estate transaction of the Church.*

Negative Example: *Board of Trustees in a Church in the Hartford Connecticut area is deliberating on a very important decision concerning a major real estate purchase. There is a notorious Board member who is known for misusing Board authority, manipulating By-laws and other beaucratic powers to advance his or her agenda. So, because this person is not the right ingredient, the church cannot make a* *decision and is in jeopardy of losing the cash it put down for the real estate transaction.*

Flexible Structures

A church or non-profit organization is in the business of serving society and the community in which they occupy. Though the foundational mission, creed or purposes may not change, Board of Trustee structures and members must be flexible in delivering managerial strategies and direction with flexibility. In Board of Trustee leadership there must exist some level of flexibility. According to Munejohn (2015) transformational leadership is more effective than transactional leadership in showing production on organizational efficiency and performance among Churches or Non-profit organizations. In order to be flexible Boards should exhibit these the following characteristics;

A. Each Board member must be open to non-traditional methods in deploying the organizations mission and purposes. Again, you are a servant of the organization

B. Each Board member must be open to other members' suggestions in delivering managerial strategy and organizational direction.

C. Each Board member must always put the Organization above themselves. In many Churches and non-profit organizations personal agendas become more important than organizational mission.

As Board of trustee member in a Church or Non-profit organization you have the power of influence and affect governance in a positive or negative way (Bhavesh, Lorne, Hazel, & Bart, 2015). Let`s be flexible and use our power for good.

Positive Example: Board of Trustees in a Church in the Long Island, New York area have a changing congregational demographic. They meet with the Pastor and Leadership and decide to make some major managerial decisions to address this congregational change. They made the following changes; 1. Amend the By-laws to reflect the more changing congregation and 2. bring in a Board Consultant to advise the membership on more effective best practices in Board management and execution.

Negative Example*: There are members on the Board that are not open to change. The Board of Trustees from an executive level are not willing to be flexible to make major adjustments in the By-laws that represent the growing change in the demographics of* *the church. Eventually, as the months and years go by the congregation dwindles down and becomes less engaged in the inadequate ways the heart beat is reaching the church.*

A Ship That Moves

The Church or Non-profit organization must always be focus on serving the public good of the community. A Church or Non-profit organization that is on the move is constantly looking for measurements of achievement that show that the organization is moving forward. When a ship stands still it is just an object that is floating in the water, but a ship that moves create waves and movement in water. What is your Board of Trustees' or leadership? Is it just a ship that stand still or is it creating waves in the water? Is it making waves of change in your local, regional or international community? Is the Board thinking of innovative ways to partner with local organizations, municipalities, businesses and etc. to further the mission and purposes of the organization? Ask yourself is your Board of Trustees' A Ship that Moves or are they one that stands still?

If your Board is one that moves you will exhibit the following;

A. Yearly outside Board training and development

B. Monthly, Quarterly or Yearly bench marks. Again these are all based on the size of your organization

C. No stinking thinking. Saying this is how we always did it and not open to change

Positive example: *The forward thinking Board of Trustees of a Church in Metro Indianapolis has voted to make sure that every year that they have two major professional services performed every year to move the organization forward. The first one is to conduct a Financial Review or Audit on the organization and Board of Trustee training.*

Negative example: *The Board of Trustees of a Church in Raleigh-Durham, North Carolina area have continued to operate*

without updated managerial best practices

and decides not to get an Financial Audit or

Review and yearly Board of Trustee

training. After, twelve months of not taking

the advice of the Senior Pastor and other

Leadership, after the IRS gets an anonymous

tip by a disgruntled member of the

congregation, they conduct and Audit and

find that there has been a misappropriation

of money. The Church is then forced to pay

a fine.

Conclusion

In conclusion you are a change agent, uphold your duty, serve and watch your influence be shown through the organization. As a Board of Trustee you are a vital part of the team, this team includes Presidents, Senior Pastors, Congregations and the community. Remember, the team is meant to work together to bring forth a common goal. The power of the Board is not to be abused for selfish gain but to be used as a tool to bring forth growth, change and progress. It's time to take that new wine and place it into New Wine Skins.

Notes

_____

_____

_____

_____

_____

_____

_____

_____

_____

_____

_____

_____

_____

_____

_____

_____

_____

_____

_____

_____

_____

_____

Milestones

Day 30

Day 90

Day 180

References

Herraiz, Marta, et al. "Analysis of wine distillates made from muscat grapes (Pisco) by multidimensional gas chromatography and mass spectrometry." *Journal of Agricultural and Food Chemistry* 38.7 (1990): 1540-1543.

Butler, R., & Wilson, D. C. (2015). *Managing voluntary and non-profit organizations: Strategy and structure.* Routledge Revivals.

McKinney, J. B. (2015). *Effective financial management in public and nonprofit agencies.* ABC-CLIO.

Bhavesh S. P., Lorne D. Booker, Hazel Melanie Ramos, Chris Bart, (2015) "Mission statements and performance in non-profit organisations", Corporate Governance, Vol.

15 Iss: 5, pp.759 – 774. DOI:
http://dx.doi.org/10.1108/ CG-07-2015-0098

Bai, G. (2013). How do board size and
occupational background of directors
influence social performance in for-profit
and non-profit organizations? Evidence from
California hospitals. *Journal of business
ethics, 118*(1), 171-187. DOI:
10.1007/s10551-012-1578-x

Muenjohn, N. (2015). Transformational
leadership: The influence of culture on the
leadership behaviors of expatriate
managers. *international Journal of Business
and information, 2*(2).

About the Author

Damien S. Fields stands at the forefront of an emerging Consulting firm. He has spent a number of years evangelizing an industry that is shifting to the use of innovative technology, and new rules and regulations within the Accounting, Taxation and Consulting arena. Damien holds a MBA in Entrepreneurship/Finance and bachelor's degree in Community Service/Business.

As a calculated risk-taker with strong finance and consulting industry knowledge, Damien has made an imprint on the way professional services to customers are delivered; Through the motto of "Your

Business is our business", HME has built a client base from Connecticut to far West as Arizona that understands his passion for helping other business succeed. His desire is to help others to achieve their business goals and in doing so... he will have achieved his.